Apple Orchard

SHAHLA LATIFI

Copyright © 2017 Shahla Latifi

All rights reserved.

Title: **Apple Orchard**
Author: **Shahla Latifi**
Editor: **Kristen Hamilton**
Cover Design: **Robin E. Vuchnich**
Publisher: **Supreme Art**, Reseda, CA
ISBN: **978-1942912347**
Library Congress Control Number: **2017919136**

DEDICATION

To those who inspired me

ACKNOWLEDGMENTS

I am thankful to all my readers, who spend their valuable time reading my poetry.

CONTENTS

Apple Orchard 1
A Grand Poem 3
Wings of A Book 4
The Chapel of Love 5
Raw Pleasure 7
Love Is Kindness 9
Pleasurable Dream 10
Travelers of Life 12
Age 13
Broken Youth 14
Surreal Reality 16
Winter 18
Freedom 19
Good Intentions 20
Horizon 21
Memories 23
Light of Wisdom 24
Troubled Storm 25
Farkhunda 26
Harmony 28
A Sonnet of Love 29
When You Are A Mother 31
Entirety of Love 33
Cobbles of Hardship 35
Glory of Lights 37
Short Poems-1 38
Short Poems-2 40
Short Poems-3 42
Short Poems-4 44
Short Poems-5 46
Demands of Sanity 48
The Heart of Humanity 49
Mozart 51
Peace 52
Transparent 53
A Refugee Child 54
Currents of Unfairness 56
A Brisk Walk 57
Carefree 58
An Imaginary Man 60
Victims of War 61
Barren Heart 63
Dance of Happiness 65
Night Breeze 67

APPLE ORCHARD

I miss you
Do you miss me
Do you feel ecstasy when you think of me
Free as a bird in the garden with sweet air
And thoughts that are so mellow and tender
Like the love of redemption with no greed

I miss you
Do you miss me
As spring that waits for autumn to turn white
And the season could return to the arms of colorful delights

I miss you
Do you miss me
Like the honeyeater in the apple orchard
In a wish for the scent of the ripe pomegranate tree

I miss you with feelings that connect
Love and feminine worries into the feelings of the heart
That are content with security

And by time
Again and again
Stable as the sun
As throbbing as the fish that swims in the stream
Free as the wind that dances around a cherry blossom tree

And as pure as the moon lit by the sun
That mystifies the strength of transaction

I miss you
And I'm thinking of you
With the traces of my feelings
With the hidden roaring of intimacy

Shahla Latifi
July 15, 2016

A GRAND POEM

"I love you like a grand poem."
Like a poem that reflects the beauty of night
In the arms of a sleeping lover
Through his content breath
In the sweet scent of satisfaction

"I love you like a grand poem."
A poem that reflects the beauty of a day
Under a silky sheet of roses
An admirer seeks his love
And holds on to the feelings of satisfaction
With her aroma on his mind

"I love you like a grand poem."
A poem that reflects the art of pleasure
In the midst of two bodies
That brings the joy of contentment
And as a grand poem
With amusement of its meaning
That awakens our sleepy thoughts with the lush feelings of dawn

Shahla Latifi
August 30, 2015

WINGS OF A BOOK

Books – The land of imagination is so clear yet complex
I could fly on the wings of a book
On the layers of dreamy clouds
I could sing from my heart in the land of freedom with no disguise
I can meet a prefect hero
An elegant queen
In the fascinating layers of pleasure
Face to face
In books I can solve any puzzle
Heal any pain
And wipe out any tear
I will find hope
Pleasures
Truthfulness
And nothing of despair
In books I will sink deep into with love
That I adore
For years to come and more

Shahla Latifi
April 15, 2015

THE CHAPEL OF LOVE

The chapel of love was peaceful
All the angels were sleeping on the wings of happiness
It was a beautiful December day

Inside the chapel
A violinist was playing

The soft melodies
That carried me on the wings of pleasure in a garden so green
A garden
That was covered
With melodious sonnets and the
Contrast of light and sound
Of Beethoven's symphony No. 5
And Mozart 3.'s sweet delight
In a garden with soft passages of love
On a breezy night
With two lovers
When the wind dances around them
And the moon that smiled with no ominous clouds upon its face

And in chapel of love
Guests sat calmly
With no laughter, no sound of any kind, anxiously waiting
To see the bride
The beautiful bride with skin like ripe olives

From an olive grove that faced the Mediterranean sea

Her hair was soft
And flowing
Under a vanilla orchid tree

And to see the groom
A man with a bright smile on his face

Very softly

Suddenly in the chapel
The silence was broken
By emotions and with the footsteps of couples that entered one by one

Their heads high with pride
Their hearts excited with the sweetness
Of a bond that is divine
They held each others hands
Like the cold branches of vines
That shiver softly for the warmth of sun above

And finally when they stood face to face
In the chapel of love

People smiled
And the couple smiled
To celebrate a togetherness
To celebrate the beginning of incredible journey of life
As man and wife
Hand to hand

Shahla Latifi
January 10, 2016

RAW PLEASURE

My thoughts are swaying in my heart
When I think of the warmth of one's skin on mine
I tremble with that thought
I smile with my lips tight
And I taste raw pleasure
I see the full moon covers
The dimensions of a small bedroom
In a cabin in the sky

My thoughts are swaying in my heart
When I feel a pleasurable moment
That consumes my femininity entirely
With the gentle touch of a firm hand that feels mine

My thoughts are swaying in my heart
My heart is beating with excitement
When I see a hummingbird settles on a fresh summer peach
To nibble the juice of life as a treat

My thoughts are swaying in my heart
When I wonder the sweetness of his touch
The caresses of his arms
And the heat of his lips
When he whispers his devotion into my heart

My thoughts are swaying in my heart

With the view of unity
That brings the mellow sound of a woman

With the sensual rhythm of poetry in the arms of a man
In the majestic moment of relief

Shahla Latifi
May 10, 2016

LOVE IS KINDNESS

Love is kindness
Love is compassion
Love is the tenderness in our thoughts
During a tragic event
Love is a kiss
That is set upon your cheek by your mother
Love is the aroma
That pours pleasure in the air
Love is a strong wind
That carries clouds of suspicion
Behind the smoky mountains of Neverland
Love is a word
That brings the broken pieces of harmony together
Love is a connection from your heart to mine
With no boundaries
Love is happy occurrence
That brings people to laughter
Love is a bird that flies high as she can with no fear
Love is a surreal thought
That encourages hearts to care
Love is me
Love is you
Love is every one that could comprehend every aspect of war and hatred
With the grand feeling of forgiveness with care

Shahla Latifi
09-15-2015

PLEASURABLE DREAM

Dark and dewy in a drizzly cold evening
He loved to be cherished
In the shadow of his thoughts
He imagined a pleasurable dream
With restless whispers and moans
He is lying under a willow tree
In peace
As harmony of the sea

With a smile of delight
He reached out to her with adoration, without hesitation
She stepped in the warmth of his affection

He tumbled like a leaf
The hidden moon glanced down
Stars twinkled overhead in a half-cloudy sky
The breeze calming
And the bliss of love began to stream

She smiled softly
All of the touch
The laughter
The whispers
And the secrets in their glances
Faded away into the sunset
And the night left the love nest

APPLE ORCHARD

For the morning to rise above

With the oasis of serenity amid troubles

Shahla Latifi
January 1, 2017

TRAVELERS OF LIFE

We are the travelers of life
Each one of us takes a different path
To differ our selves as individuals
In the challenging circle of life

One takes the straight path
That is safe, yet barren of happiness

The other takes a path so abstruse and knotty
Yet rewarding and tight

Some take the same path as the the one next to him
Without defining his own taste buds

And a few
Stay in one path without rising the bars
Of effusion and gains

But despite all
We are all connected in one circle
With hopes
Wishes
True sentiments
Likes and dislikes as human
The most complex race of all

Shahla Latifi
August 18, 2015

AGE

Age
The defying beauty of life stands tall
On any day
On any night
In every cold
In every warmth
Inside of the cocoon of life
To guide us
To carry us
And to make us settle
On the restless journey of life

Shahla Latifi
June 15, 2016

BROKEN YOUTH

The young girl with colorless cheeks
Her hands as rough as the winter cobbled streets
Her hair as soiled as the roots of an old tree
Her stomach as empty as a small hungry baby
Her eyes linger on the ceiling of a small room
That contains nothing
But empty shelves
An old rug
And a few books
She wished she was able to read them all
Piece by piece

As she lies quietly
Like the flower's bed under her small window
She thinks of her youth that was wasted
Her heart that was abandoned
Her imagination that has faded
And of her parents who parted
And she thinks of all her pain inside
Since the day she was given away as a bride
To an old man
With tears in her eyes
And her right hand on her heart
She suddenly realizes that her path has already been chosen
A path that's very narrow, yet straight
And she has to grant the wishes

APPLE ORCHARD

Of her unborn child that breathes inside of her
For better life
With determination and strength

Shahla Latifi
August 4, 2015

SURREAL REALITY

Age doesn't define me
As I do not set goals
As I mainly go with the flow

With no fear
I can fly charmingly
To the peak of any dream
With my spirits high

As the moonlit shines on the voyage
Bold
But oblivious
I could fly on the wings of a royal falcon
Of any desire
Willingly
Age doesn't define me

The melodious sound of affection
That runs through my beating heart
That's alive with hope
With a taste of surreal reality
With a fascination
Raw and adoring
That defines me

Age doesn't define me

APPLE ORCHARD

The real meaning of life
That flows in my blood
That runs through the garden of wisdom
Defines me
A smile of satisfaction blossoming on my face
Defines me
Age doesn't define me

Shahla Latifi
July 1, 2016

WINTER

Winter has arrived
To make the bald eagles to fly up to their maximum power
And to dive in the unfrozen lakes
Or a river
With the heat of their strength
To catch a satisfying meal

Winter has arrived
To fill up all the barren wells
So tomorrow's gardens can grow fresh roses

Winter has arrived
For the wolf to explore deep in the snow
With his extraordinary sense of survival

Winter is not cruel
It's not demanding
And it's not here
To make us suffer

Winter is a blessing of nature
That awakens the love of life in heart of spring

Shahla Latifi
December 20, 2015

FREEDOM

Freedom is at our fingertips
When we free a bird from the cage

Freedom is in a smile
When we comfort an orphan child

Freedom allows our dreams to take flight

Freedom is in the air, and in the layers of a stream

Freedom is not a treasure
A possession, or a jewel

Freedom is a happy wind that blows our hair
Around an apple orchard in spring

Shahla Latifi
November 25, 2015

GOOD INTENTIONS

When I am down
Down with the tears of disappointments
That bring me a profound silence
With an enthusiastic smile all around

When I am down in the darkness of shadow misery
Bring me candles for the window to see joy and ecstasy

When I am down
Very down
With the shivering feelings of loneliness in the middle of night
Bring me a comforter that has soaked in my mother's scent

When I am down
In the strong wind of a stormy day with my eyes shut
Bring me your strong hands to guide me through whatever lies ahead

When I am down with the secret thoughts of heartbreak
Bring me love on the palm of your good intentions
For this injured heart to mend

Shahla Latifi
November 30, 2015

HORIZON

As the new year approaches
She is overwhelmed
And she is a little cold
With feelings of abandonment from all the injured souls In the hands of darkness and despair

Around the world

As the new year approaches
She is nervous with conscious perception
Of a mysterious feeling inside
That all the wishes of children of Earth
Will not be granted

As the new year approaches
The lady in green is worried
About the dark circumstances
With which all sweet dreams suffer

She is worried
That she is going to fail again to reach her expectations
To end all the war
To introduce humankind to an unfolded mystery
Of how we can survive
How we can mend the broken boundaries
And how we all can triumph

Before the horizon succumbs to the dark side
For all eternity

Shahla Latifi
December 28, 2015

MEMORIES

*Memories are like rain drops
That soothe our minds
By the touch of a loving pleasure*

*Memories are like an untold story
That lives in our hearts
With a desire and need to share*

*Good memories are like an uplifting memoir
That contains the bold lines of sweet love poems
That carries you on the imaginative wings of love and enthusiasm
Bold and fair*

*Bad memories
Are like a sad adventure
In which you have been told to bury your thoughts
Under a harsh brick wall*

*And we all are the players of life
Spinning around all of our memories
Good and bad
Sweet and bitter
Happy and unwanted
To comfort our hearts In a balanced act of wisdom
With care*

*Shahla Latifi
September 2, 2015*

LIGHT OF WISDOM

When I see the light of wisdom
Is not languishing in sorrow

When I see that every one has enough to eat

When I see there is no soul
At the mercy of a vicious deed

When I see the lights of comfort
Shining through the night

When I see there is no child hopeless
With an injured mind
Then I would think
The glory of God still exists
In mankind

Shahla Latifi
August 10, 2014

TROUBLED STORM

A flower needs care
With the hands of kindness of her mother
And the caring voice
Of her father
Who reads to her the song of patience and wisdom
During starry nights

But when a storm arises
And the storm hits the little garden of peace
That flower dies
The care dies
And the voice of wisdom dies along within her

In a moment of chaos
During a troubled storm
From heart of angry sea

Shahla Latifi
November 10, 2015

FARKHUNDA

Farkhunda had a soul with layers of pain
That covered her hopes and desires
As a woman that she couldn't be

Her eyes glistening with tears
Her heart shattered by despair
For she knew that her life as an ill woman was not easy

She wanted a rescuer
A guide, a helping hand to give her hope
Comfort, and a friendly smile
To assure her that everything will get better

But instead, on that cold day of spring
Her dreams and hopes were shattered
With stones of disbelief, betrayal
And lies

Her body was taken out of her soul
With undeserved cruelty
And no respect for her life

I wonder how she felt in those moments
Tortured to a painful death

Did she still believe in God?

APPLE ORCHARD

Was she calling to her mother from inside?
Or did she know that the cruelty of human race
Is above all her good wishes?

I wonder with the tears in my heart
If she knew that compassion
Is a seldom gift that humanity bestows

I wonder if we can ever be able to rebuild
The broken compassion in our hearts
And let humanity shine like a burning star

Shahla Latifi
June 3, 2015

HARMONY

Harmony, it matters
Among all living souls
In a household
Where all the essence grows

Harmony, it matters
At the end of a relation
That spirals our thought with unjustified pain and anguish
On a happy, bright Sunday morning
When the love and happiness glow

Harmony, it matters
At the start of a friendship
That excites us with delight
When the storm comes blowing
On an icy cold night

Harmony, it matters
And it's a gift that would shine
In the darkness with no hope
To bridge all of our wisdom
For inner strength to grow

Shahla Latifi
October 20, 2016

A SONNET OF LOVE

If I were to have a lover
I would desire him to be like warmth of sun on my skin
When the world is frozen under my feet

If I were to have a lover
In my time of need
I would step in a garden full of lively flowers observing
As they smile at me

If I were to have a lover
His gifts would contain glorious feelings
As soft as the feather of a dove for my treat

If I were to have a lover
He would relax my mind with the sweet words of endearment
As I travel into a sonnet of love, lavishly

If I were to have a lover
A lover who could bring me joy
I would frequently invite courage
To the doorsteps of my mind

If I were to have a lover
A lover so genuine
A lover so compassionate
I would look up at the sky with a passionate and content mind

Ready to find my true destiny

Shahla Latifi
January 10, 2016

WHEN YOU ARE A MOTHER

When you are a mother
Your world exists around your children
Your happiness is tied to their laughter
Giggles
Hopes
Dreams

When you are a mother
Your tears of joy fall on the footsteps of their gladness
And the tears of worry follow the trace of their sadness
Disappointments
And heartbreaks

When you are a mother
You'll find your true self in your child's eyes
You will find comfort with their touch in your arms
And you'll find treasure
In the sweetness of their voice

When you are a mother
You are dignified as a person
And given a purpose of sharing your days and dreams
With their laughter and more

When you are a mother
Your needs are secondary

But your love expands from ordinary
To extraordinary
Until you become whole

Shahla Latifi
March 12, 2015

ENTIRETY OF LOVE

I need you
I need your attention
The certainty of your love
To seek out a new life with my presence at night
I need your emotions to wrap me within itself

In the deepest layers of needs
And my need has no greed

I assure you
I need your passion to justify me as a woman
As a dignified truce

I need you when the sense of darkness hovers over the depth of my soul
I need you for me
For my worrisome thoughts at night

I need you to take me to the height of your power
I need you like the leaves that bloom on a tree under the sun
Like the stream surrounding a new life
With purity and the essence of love

I need your open arms
At the peak of my illusion
In the darkest moments of my day

I need you as the sun touches the moon for its transaction of light
When the birds awaken
In the sleepy meadow on the mountaintop

I need you like fresh air blows the power of love around nature
I need you on my skin like clean blossoms with the touch of morning dew
I need you
As time moves from spring to autumn
When wild geese are dancing in the icy lake next to a winter garden
With a touch of an entirety of love

Shahla Latifi
December 1, 2016

COBBLES OF HARDSHIP

There was a time
When I was attached to the strings of pain
Inside a cocoon of loneliness

I felt
Abandoned
With no window to see outside
With the feeling
Of hopelessness in mind
And fear in my heart

I started to lose the essence of my well being inside
One foggy night
With a clear thought
And sickly body

I looked up at the small reflection of my soul in the cracked ceiling of the cocoon
That lit up with the ray of the moon
I saw my soul
So frail
Defeated
And unhappy
As an orphaned child

I felt that weakness conquered my motivation
And I sensed that my self-worth was broken

On the cobbled stones of hardship
Piece by piece

I also saw a fragment of a little girl
Whom once was
Driven
Passionate
And so alive
But imprisoned in the cell of a broken cocoon
With no fresh air to breathe
No power to scream
And no strength to go on

I started to cry
And with a throbbing heart
I felt this disconnection of myself
From the pain that I've been feeling
For so long

Suddenly
I felt relieved
And my courage was awakened
And I felt the urge to recollect
My strength
And my wisdom
As a torch of guidance
To the passage to freedom
From the cocoon

Shahla Latifi
October 20, 2015

GLORY OF LIGHTS

My heart flies with happiness
Like the thoughts of a free bird
That greets me on a foggy dawn

I smile with the happy bird
As she settles on the warmth of my palm

With a stroke of a fingertip on the layers of her soft feathers
She closes her eyes
And lays her small head on the cushion of my hand

I kiss her softly
She stirs
And she opens her eyes
With a loving demeanor
To look at me

Suddenly
She starts humming a beautiful melody of sunshine
A melody that brings love to any cold feelings
In a foggy dawn

A melody that makes the sun rise with a projection of peace
And for the dawn to engage with glory
Of prairie lights once again

Shahla Latifi
March 2, 2016

SHORT POEMS-1

My heart
Cannot be settled in your arms
When my body senses
An untrustworthy aroma

And my mind is hungry and intrigued,
Seeking the meaning of "love"
In an enchanted journey
Through the valley of pleasure or pain with trust

****

If I was a hummingbird
With my small feathers

That are wet from the rain
I would fly up to you

I would sit on your shoulder
Shaking off all the rain water
Onto your heart

In your memories
And in your mind
With the equation of love in drops

APPLE ORCHARD

****

I have found treasure in nature
The glory of life

And I have found the meaning of being alive
With the dewy flowers of dawn

****

A ray
Of good days
Is a pathway
To see a brighter tomorrow
From a small opening
Of despair

So
With the keen eyes of enthusiasm
Find that light
To gain self awareness
And to create your happiness
With ambition
Not fear

Shahla Latifi
2015

SHORT POEMS-2

There will be a day
When light will shine
Freedom will laugh
And peace will settle on everybody's chest up high

****

If I find the true essence of love
In my fingertips
Like a ray of sun
That peeks from the windowsill

I will open all of my senses
To a fascinating journey
Around love and trust

****

Anxiety
Tiredness
Depression
Worries
Despair
And the feeling of abandonment
Are the shadowy disguise of broken hopes

APPLE ORCHARD

****

Hold the moon in your thoughts
Whenever you are alone
In the darkness

****

My lips were pursed as flower buds

My eyes closed in a moment of sinking

Into his eyes
My skin felt warm with his touch

When I saw myself lying next to him
On a garden bench

His hair on my face
My hands on his shoulders
His lips closed on mine
And the intense rhythms of my heart
So tender

Suddenly
I opened my eyes with a sparkle of virtue
And suppressed all his greed into his soul
That I am a "woman"
A woman of her own rights
A woman to be cherished and to be loved
Not only to be kissed and fantasized

Shahla Latifi
2015

SHORT POEMS-3

I'll celebrate the new year with colors
With colors of hopes and dreams
Life, liberty, and the pursuit of happiness
And with the colors of prosperity and peace In the world

Shahla Latifi
December 29, 2015

****

Cherish my heart
So I can fly on the wings
Of a dream

Shahla Latifi
December 15, 2015

****

My youth
Was like the delicacy and strength of a ribbon
That connected my body
Mind
And soul

APPLE ORCHARD

Into an enchanted melody
Of dreams

Shahla Latifi
October 15, 2015

****

I grew up in a village
With fresh air around me
Green grass under my feet
The apple trees behind a silver street
And they were all connecting my soul
With a happy bumblebee
That was dancing carefree
On the top of a young branch
In peace

Shahla Latifi
September 29, 2015

****

A woman
She is not just a face
She is a mind
A flare of wisdom accompanies her thoughts

A woman is not just a face
She is a reflection of light
That strives
For the search of the true meaning of happiness
With a great wish of equality

Shahla Latifi
November 18, 2015

SHORT POEMS-4

Palm trees, the free umbrellas of nature
A wave of peace to remember
Layered with freedom
Miraculously, a sense of liberty
Binds the spirit of a palm tree and I together

****

I remember the night
The starry night
When a sudden gust of forbidden love
Danced around you and I

I remember the night
The starry night
When the vast horizon fell from the sky
I was sitting in front of a small garden listening to the breeze
The rhythmic sound of wind played melodically

I remember the night
The starry night
When you faced the sunset
Your glistening eyes looking at me
Nightingales were singing
As the dusk turned into night

APPLE ORCHARD

****

Tulips, the free-spirited beauties
Uneasy in the hands of stormy nights
Lay softly in the arms of a majestic land
In peace among the chaos
Peaceful with the joy that rises at sunset
Sways with the emotion of the breeze; divine

Shahla Latifi
August 2016

SHORT POEMS-5

When he touched her face with affection
She trembled

When he smiled at her
She blushed

When he glanced into her eyes
The warmth of her heart awakened
And the purity of her existence bloomed
With the aroma of young love

Suddenly
She smiled at the garden with the feeling of fulfillment
With the urge to soar like a butterfly
To spread her wings on the green garden of life
Soaked with the energy of love

Shahla Latifi
August 15, 2016

****

On the shore of intimacy
The sea breeze rises
The sky looks down upon the sunrise

APPLE ORCHARD

The thunder of love roars
When two hearts come together
And two bodies are joined as one
By soaking up the waves of pleasure
On a heavenly night on the sea

Shahla Latifi
August 26, 2015

DEMANDS OF SANITY

I cry when I am broken
Unwanted and overwhelmed
But there is no shame in crying

I cry
Like an unhappy bird with an injured wing under a tree
I cry like the roaring thunder in the midst of a spring day
I cry like a child
When a disaster takes his mother away
I cry, and I cry
I cry softly

At times, I cry soundly with no demands of sanity
I cry in a moment of depression with an aura of gloominess
To release me
From the cold clutches of insanity
And to cultivate my unconfident mind
With a new smile
And the exhilarating energy
That revolves around me

Shahla Latifi
June 19, 2016

THE HEART OF HUMANITY

I believe the bliss of love can join
The enthusiastic dance of peace for eternity

I believe in the goodness
That still exists
like the ray of redemption in a guilty heart
That is remorseful, sad, and sorry

I believe the returning strength
In the body of an abounded wall
That has betrayed
Beaten and broken
By the hands of war and greed

I believe children can smile
With no fear of hopelessness
Once again
They will cheerfully dance on the meadows
They will read aloud with their hearts as open as the sun
They will laugh at their wittiness

They will form friendships with colorful flowers
And they will find their way to the moon
Which will lighten their dreams
With her soft and loving light of perfection

And to grab the inspiration from the moon
To broaden their horizons beyond the sea

I believe the morality of life
With the unbalanced force of imperfection

So perplexed
Yet alive
It's going to find its way
To the heart of humanity
Without boundary

Shahla Latifi
June 25, 2016

MOZART

On a sunny day
In the bare prairie of my delusion
I'm thinking of your music

With the unbounded spirit of soothing melody in my ears
I'm thinking of you alive, Mozart

The rhythmic glory of the piano
In the layers of "Piano Sonata No 11"
So divine
So immortal
With a blissful imagination of unity
Brings my heart close to you, Mozart

Shahla Latifi
February 1, 2017

PEACE

Peace
The most valuable commodity of life is missing
In the layers of a world filled with bitterness
Under the clouds of animosity
In the hearts of war-damaged victims
In the eyes of humanity's greed and cruelty

Peace
The most valuable commodity of life is missing
From our hearts
In the dust of disbelief, that swirls around us
With nothing but despair and agony

Peace
The most valuable commodity of life is missing
The hands of prejudice and inequality drove it away

Let us find that precious commodity together
Till its spirit gives us courage
Till peace
The most valuable commodity of life
Returns triumphantly

Shahla Latifi
June 25, 2016

TRANSPARENT

I am as transparent as a crystal vase
With stems of roses within its heart

That reflects the beauty of nature and the meaning of life
Brilliant yet perplexed

I am transparent like the moonlight
That shines through the darkness
And connects with my thoughts

I am transparent like a child's giggle
That buries an innocent lie into his heart

I am as transparent as a wish
That grants the gift of sacrifice

My transparency is always bright
Though my surroundings may change
It always sees the untold truth within my heart

Shahla Latifi
August 10, 2016

A REFUGEE CHILD

Most of the Afghan refugees who fled the war in Afghanistan lived in refugee camps near the Pakistan-Afghanistan border. The situation inside the refugee camps was dire, and thousands of refugee children faced life-threatening conditions. This poem is dedicated to those children and any refugee children around the world.

I am a refugee child
I am a flower that has been cut from the stem

I am a refugee child
I am a child who is caught up in the middle of a frightful war

When the night covers the vile world with its dark coat
When I am resting on the muddy ground next to an unlocked door
I feel myself again
I feel like a child that could smile in peace
That could go to an enchanted dream

In daylight when I hear the roar of the crowd
When I feel the sun's warmth on my skin
When I listen to hungry babies' sad cry for help
When an injured man moans in pain

When I look around the valley of abandoned dreams
Full of anguish and astounding poverty
As we are all cramped in a cell of depression
With no hope and no fresh air to breathe

APPLE ORCHARD

My soul becomes cold
My heart gets lost in despair so deep

But when the nights fall softly upon us
I sense the essence of hope that rushes joyfully in me
Suddenly I feel like a child
A child with a desire to be free

Shahla Latifi
September 1, 2016

CURRENTS OF UNFAIRNESS

In the tender age of womanhood I heard
I sensed
I felt the pain

The unforgivable currents of unfairness and injustice
That settled on the shore of my body and soul

In the tender age of womanhood
I cried
And keenly wished that tomorrow would be kinder to me

Behind the wall of broken dreams
A tree of energy grew each day
With that tree, I learned
I explored my mind

From the crack of dawn to the layers of moonless cloudy nights
To grow
To love
To laugh
To give
To hug
To fall
And to fly up like an eagle
As sincere as the light of dawn upon a green meadow

Shahla Latifi
July 15, 2016

A BRISK WALK

A brisk walk on a fall day
That awakens the love of nature in your heart
Enlightens the new life with a sense of freedom in your mind
Is a heavenly gift to remember

A brisk walk at night
When the stars shine down on you
And the moon illuminates your path
Is a heavenly gift to remember

A brisk walk with your love
On any breezy day
On any bright afternoon
On any rainy evening

On any long, sad day that you leave your worries behind
Is a heavenly gift to remember

A brisk walk in the happy time
When excitement covers the unsettled feelings of the melancholy past
Is how to treat life

Shahla Latifi
October 25, 2016

CAREFREE

Touch me with your senses
So I can fly on the wings of a dream
In rapturous ecstasy

Laugh with me from your heart
So I can run into the thickness of a dream
As a nightingale sings at night, carefree

Hold me in your thoughts
So I can sway in the arms of a dream
Like a willow tree in spring, lazily

Sing for me
So I can hear your whispers
As sweet sensation of love melody

Kiss me with your eyes open
So I can dance in the trembling hands of a passion
As the moonlight gleams mysteriously

Eat with me
So I can taste the aroma of a fresh apple
From your lips romantically

Breathe with me
Through the delicate layers of unknown happiness

APPLE ORCHARD

In the thickest clouds of sadness
With your love, patiently

Shahla Latifi
January 4, 207

AN IMAGINARY MAN

When you are in love
With an imaginary man
Who smiles at you without hesitance
Who looks at you in silence
And who gives you
Pleasure with unspoken words of affection
You feel alive
And you feel liberated from the anguish of abandonment

When you are in love with an imaginary man
With a mind of gumption
That excites you
That grows your feelings
In the days and the nights
With the flow of sanctity into awakening desire
He could devour you
This is a beautiful sense of love

Shahla Latifi
December 1, 2016

VICTIMS OF WAR

While little Alan was sleeping in his mother's arms at dawn
On a cramped boat on the Mediterranean Sea
His mother was still
She knew her path was going to be rough

Not smooth like the stream of light, pure and clear
But as a warrior in her heart
She was determined
To carry her beloved children to safety

The ocean was alert and the waves were quivering
And each wave danced in a circular motion above the sea

Fishes
Big and small
From the depth of the water held on the moving waves
To greet the visitors with the waves' transmitting energy

Children were soundlessly asleep
Men were nervous
Women were preoccupied with motherly instinct and anxiety

Suddenly
The boat unsettled
Moved to one side
And the unexpected sound of fear covered the sea

Water panicked
Fishes jumped around the boat
And spurted water with the sad news to each other
That there was going to be another
Grievous loss at the sea

Everything went silent
And still
Only the wavering sound of the sea
That laid her trembling hand
On her aching heart
To pray for the victims of war

For the seekers of freedom who took bold chances
To grab the sliver of a free land
In their fingertips of hopes
Willingly

Shahla Latifi
September 5, 2015

BARREN HEART

He abandoned me
His hands
His desire to embrace my body as the sun rises above the hilltop
And his excitement abandoned me

Suddenly dark clouds of suspicion
Lingered on the moon

And the stars left me

The warm hand of devotion
That connected the thread of love had weakened

And happiness abandoned me

The aura of the night
His barren heart
The blossoms of my needs

And the shattered hope abandoned me

When dawn rose
The glow of life shone through the window next to the sea
With a soft smile

I whispered into his ear that you had abandoned me

The rain started to pour
The room stirred up with a high breeze
The light from within my heart glowed with hope

And the still of a gloomy night abandoned me

With a roar of strength
From the depth of my ruin
Alone
I climbed the moon with highest dreams
To capture my salvation once again

Shahla Latifi
March 10, 2017

DANCE OF HAPPINESS

The aroma of black tea
Awakened my senses

The rain is pouring
My smile is widening
And my eyes are glittering with affection
Looking at my black and white cat
Who stares at me

The wind, with force and anger
Emerged from the depths of the sky
To find love
To obtain acceptance
And to taste joy with flowing rain

The rain is happy
She leans on the firm shoulder of the wind

The wind lets off steam
The rain laughs
With tears of excitement streaming down her face

Their bodies joining
And the echoing sound of pleasure can be heard from the distance

My cat, quite motionless

Rests on the soft cushion as a soundless spring breeze

And I imagine
The swaying dance of happiness by the sea

Shahla Latifi
March 30, 2017

NIGHT BREEZE

When the night breeze arises
To remove all traces of light
My heart sits deep in thought

When the moon covers the shallow end of my thoughts
A trembling hand of despair
Pulls me closer to the memory of lost love

On cloudy days when my worries are awake
I prefer to sleep in the arms of a quiet night
Calm and unafraid

In lonely moments of truth
With his memory lingering over my heart
My tremulous smile
My happy wishes
And the raw emotion that makes up the essence of my fruitful vine
Want to cry

Shahla Latifi
April 15, 2017

ABOUT THE AUTHOR

Shahla Latifi was born and raised in Kabul, Afghanistan and now she lives and writes in Florida. Her first Farsi poetry selection (*Parastootah*) was published in 2013 and her second Farsi poetry collection (*Asal Wahshi*) was published in 2015. Now her books are available through the Library of Congress online catalog. Many of her poems deal with topics such as love, humanity, equality, and happiness.

www.ingramcontent.com/pod-product-compliance
Lightning Source LLC
Chambersburg PA
CBHW032211040426
42449CB00005B/548